Reading
STREET
Grade **2**

Scott Foresman

Decodable
Readers 16-30
Volume 2

PEARSON

Scott
Foresman

Editorial Offices: Glenview, Illinois • Parsippany, New Jersey
New York, New York
Sales Offices: Needham, Massachusetts • Duluth, Georgia • Glenview,
Illinois • Coppell, Texas • Sacramento, California • Mesa, Arizona

ISBN: 0-328-14506-8

6 7 8 9 10 V054 14 13 12 11 10 09 08 07

Contents

UNIT 4

Decodable Reader 16
Lunchtime 1

Decodable Reader 17
Mike Looks for a Book 9

Decodable Reader 18
Jen's Garden 17

Decodable Reader 19
Cowboy Roy 25

Decodable Reader 20
Is It True? 33

UNIT 5

Decodable Reader 21
Hobbies 41

Decodable Reader 22
In the Woods 49

Decodable Reader 23
Pen Pals 57

Decodable Reader 24
Phil's Zoo Fun 65

Decodable Reader 25
Fun in the Summer Sun 73

UNIT 6

Decodable Reader 26
Hide and Seek! 81

Decodable Reader 27
Mom's Surprise 89

Decodable Reader 28
I Might Be 97

Decodable Reader 29
Sandy and Randy 105

Decodable Reader 30
Hiking the Hard Way 113

Lunchtime

Written by Laura Susin
Illustrated by Darrel Loemann

Phonics Skill

Syllables: Consonant + -le

simple	table	able	purple	sparkle	handle
puddle	bundle	tickle	candle	giggle	

It's time to eat.
It is simple to set the table.
Pam is able to do it
by herself.

2

First, Pam sets purple dishes
on the table.
Pam likes purple.
Today is a nice day for purple.

Pam sets glasses on the table.
They sparkle in the sunlight.
Pam gets napkins too.
Her napkins match the purple plates.
It is fun setting the table!

Pam holds the jug of
water by the handle.
She will not spill.
There will be no puddle!

This table needs
a bundle of roses.
Won't this table smell nice?
Roses tickle Pam's nose!

Last, this table needs a candle on it.
Mom will light that candle.
After that, Mom can finish
making lunch.
Pam can't wait to eat!

The table is set.
Mom sets lunch on the table.
Pam and Mom fixed lunch as a team!
It makes Pam giggle to think
of how she was able to help.

Mike Looks for a Book

Written by Quinn Hart
Illustrated by Mia Martin

Phonics Skill

Vowels oo, u as in book, put

book(s)	look	good	looking	stood	looked
cook	cookbook	took	put	full	

Mike has a card
that he uses to get books.
What kind of book
will he look for?

Mike runs up these steps.
He sees books, books,
and more books!
Can Mike find a good book?

Mike will ask the man at this desk.
"I'm looking for a book," Mike said.
"A book? We have lots of books!
What kind do you want?" he asked.

"I am looking for a good book,"
Mike said as he stood
and looked at books.
"Maybe I'll read this book.
It will teach me how to cook!"

Mike will check out this cookbook!
The man took Mike's card
and he took Mike's book.
Then he gave the book and card
back to Mike.

14

Mike put his bag down
and took a seat.
The book was full of good
things to eat.

Mike will take his book home.
He will cook with his mom!
Mike is on his way
to being a good cook!

Jen's Garden

Written by Donyette Sanchez
Illustrated by Dan Vick

Phonics Skill
Vowel Diphthongs ou, ow /ou/

found	flower(s)	frown	brown	now	how
pound	down	shower	sprout	without	sound
out	ground	proud			

Jen found a bag of flower seeds.
What can she do with them?
Jen had a frown on her face.
Then she smiled.
She will make a flower garden!

What will she do first?
Jen will plant her seeds.
A good spot of land
is what Jen needs.

This dirt is nice and brown.
Jen digs tiny holes
for the seeds.
She will dig holes
for every single one of them!

Now the seeds can be planted.
One seed in each hole
is how it's done.
Put dirt on top,
but do not pound it down!

It's time to water each seed.
It is a shower for the flowers!
It will help them sprout.
Now they just need sunlight.

When will the flowers sprout?
Without a sound,
the flowers will poke out
of the ground and go up to the sky.

23

Jen is so proud!
Her flowers did get big.
She will pick one flower
and take it home.

Cowboy Roy

Written by Julia Parrish
Illustrated by Christopher Calvetti

Phonics Skill

Vowel Diphthongs oi, oy /oi/

Roy	choice	cowboy(s)	foil	toys	spoiled
boy	joy	voice	join	noise	

"This is the day to tell
the class what you
want to be when you grow up!
Roy, will you speak first?"
the teacher asked.

26

What will Roy be?
Roy will tell the class his choice.
He will be a cowboy!

Roy will ride his horse.
He will twirl his rope.
He will herd those cows
and keep an eye on them.

Roy will protect the cows
from wild animals.
Maybe Roy will foil a plot
if some cows run away.
He can save the herd!

Roy will give up his toys
to look after cows!
Roy is not a spoiled boy.
He thinks that being a cowboy
will bring him joy.

In his camp at night,
Roy will use his fine voice
to sing cowboy tunes
under the bright stars.

Yes! He will tell the class
how he will join other cowboys!
But Roy does not make a noise.
Roy is a very shy cowboy.

Is It True?

Written by Meera Laurent
Illustrated by Judy Calhoon

Phonics Skill

Vowel Patterns oo, ue, ew, ui

Sue	true	moo	flew	moon	clue
too	proof	drew	suit	grew	soon
zoomed					

Sue needed to see
if it is true that a
cow that went "moo"
flew over the moon.

34

Sue will read to find a clue.
This book is full of cow facts.
But not a single cow flew!

Sue read about moon facts too.
It did not give proof that cows
ever came near the moon!

Sue had another clue
about what to do.
She asked an old cow
if she had ever flown over the moon.
That cow only said, "Moo."

Sue drew a picture of this cow.
She thought that wings
would suit the cow she drew.
Her hope grew that
she might soon learn if cows flew.

Sue waited and waited for
this cow to fly by.
But she soon grew tired
and her eyes closed tight.

Just as Sue started sleeping,
what do you think went by,
flying and leaping?
That cow zoomed
right over the moon!
40

Hobbies

Written by Dennis Michaels
Illustrated by Tom Hurst

Phonics Skill

Suffixes -ly, -ful, -er, -or

gardener	gladly	peaceful	restful	painter
boldly	boastful	actor	storyteller	weekly
playful	hiker(s)	bravely	teacher	

Most people have a hobby.
A hobby is something people do
in their free time to have fun.
What hobbies can you enjoy?

Janet is a gardener.
She tends her plants gladly.
She thinks her garden is
a peaceful place.
Making plants grow is restful for Janet.

Kelvin is a painter.

He makes huge paintings.

He boldly uses bright colors.

His paintings are very good,

but Kelvin is not boastful about his skills.

Kerry is an actor.
She acts in plays.
She reads plays too.
Kerry gladly tells stories on stage
through her fine acting.

45

Ben is a storyteller too,
but he does not act on stage.
He leads a weekly story time
at a little bookstore.
Kids like his playful readings.

46

Tess is a hiker.
She has finished long trails.
She has bravely hiked up peaks.
Tess is a good teacher for new hikers.

Anything can be a hobby.
It can be dance, reading,
arts and crafts, or sports.
Just find something that makes
you happy and have fun!

48

In the Woods

Written by Paula Bilika
Illustrated by Chip Mitchall

Phonics Skill
Prefixes un-, re-, pre-, dis-

unlocks	unload	precooked	unties
unpacks	unhooks	unsafe	relight
unrolls	repack	dislikes	

Kenny and his family
like to go to the woods.
They camp in tents.
They swim in the lake
and hike in the hills.

Kenny unlocks the car.
He helps his mom pack.
Dad drives them to a good spot.
Then they unload tents,
full backpacks, and precooked food.

51

Kenny unties the ropes on the tent.
He helps his mom and dad
set up the tents.
Then Dad unpacks the food
and sets out a yummy dinner.

Kenny likes fishing at the lake.
If Dad gets a small fish, he unhooks
it and puts it back in the lake.
Those fish are too little to keep.

Mom puts water on the campfire
when they go hiking.
"It is unsafe to let it burn,"
Mom tells Kenny.
"We can relight it later."

54

At night, Kenny unrolls
his soft sleeping bag and slips in.
Sleep will feel good
after his full day
of hiking, fishing, and swimming.

When it's time to go,
Kenny helps to repack the car.
Kenny dislikes litter,
so he cleans up the campsite.
Kenny can't wait to come back!

Pen Pals

Written by Jamie Bernsen
Illustrated by Fran W. Beck

Phonics Skill
Silent Consonants kn, wr, gn, mb

write	wrote	climbed	limb	knee
wrapped	numb	knights	knots	knit
thumb	signed			

Fred has a friend named Dan.
Dan lives far away.
Fred and Dan write letters
and tell each other a lot.

58

Dan wrote a letter to Fred.
So Fred took out paper
and wrote a letter back to Dan.
He had a lot to tell him.

"I climbed a tree and
went out on a limb.
I fell and hurt my knee.
Mom wrapped it and put
ice packs on it to make it numb."

60

"After that, Mom got me
a new game with knights,
kings, and queens," Fred wrote.
"The knights ride horses."

Fred told Dan about his camping trip.
He told about the two cats
that Mom brought home.
"I like to watch them play
on the rug," Fred wrote.

Fred told Dan that he
is learning to tie knots.
His grandmother wants
to show him how to knit too.
"It looks like a fun hobby," Fred wrote.

Fred told Dan that he had
to stop writing.
"My thumb is hurting," he wrote.
He signed his letter
and added a note: "Write soon!"

Phil's Zoo Fun

Written by Alex Gardner
Illustrated by Nancy Peters

Phonics Skill
/f/ ph, gh

Phil	enough	graph	Phil's
photos	phrase	dolphin(s)	laughs

Phil likes animals.
Every summer, he and his parents
visit the city zoo.
Phil can never get enough
of seeing things at that zoo.

First, they go in the petting zoo.
Phil likes petting the horses.
He feeds them hay.
A graph posted on the gate
shows how fast horses grow.

His mom gives him a bag.
It is stuffed with food
to feed the eager goats.
Those goats eat from Phil's bag.
His dad takes photos.

Phil and his parents pet a soft
rabbit on the way out.
Next Phil visits wild animals.
He sees signs with the phrase
"No food!"

Hippos play in mud.
They look happy
by that cool stream.
Three foxes dart under bushes.
They are playing.

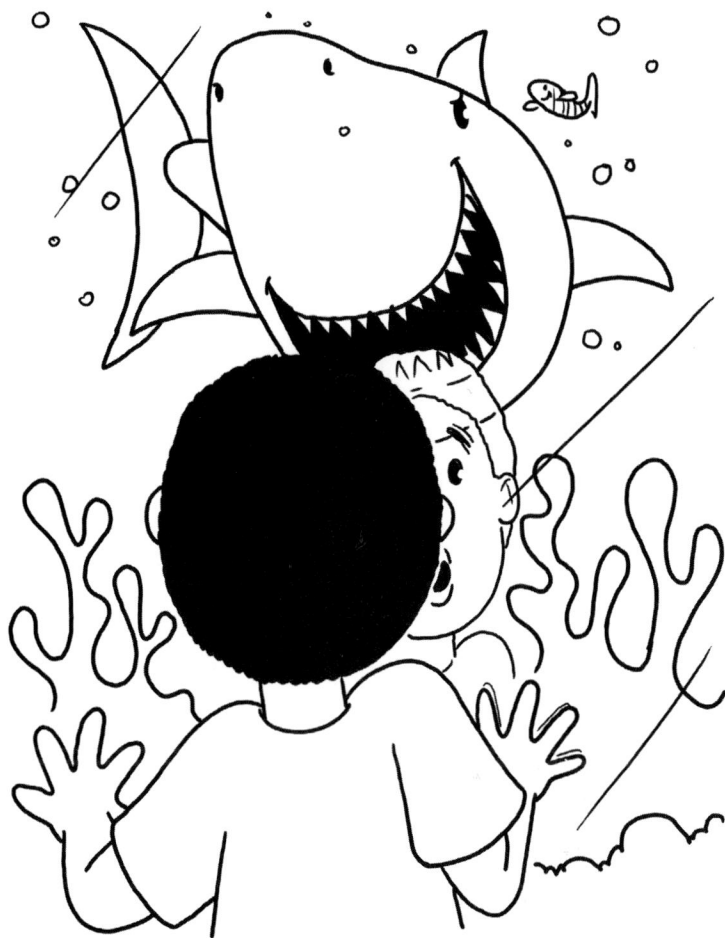

In the fish house,
Phil sees sea stars, puffer fish,
sea horses, and sharks.
Phil likes to see
the sharks getting fed.

Before the zoo closes, Phil and his
mom and dad see a dolphin show.
The zoo staff taught dolphins
to do fun tricks.
Splash! Everybody laughs.

72

Fun in the Summer Sun

Written by Maggie Yeom
Illustrated by Cherri Britze

Phonics Skill

Vowels aw, au, au(gh), al

August	all	baseball	walk
always	caught	launch	taller
fall	falls	thaw	

August is hot!
The sun shines all day.
I cannot stop playing
in the hot, hot sun.

74

Baseball is the best game
to play in the summer.
We walk or run from base to base.
We always know our team is good.
We win a lot and have fun.

Down at that lake
I caught a fish.
We tried to launch a boat,
but it did not float.
Maybe we'll make a new boat!

76

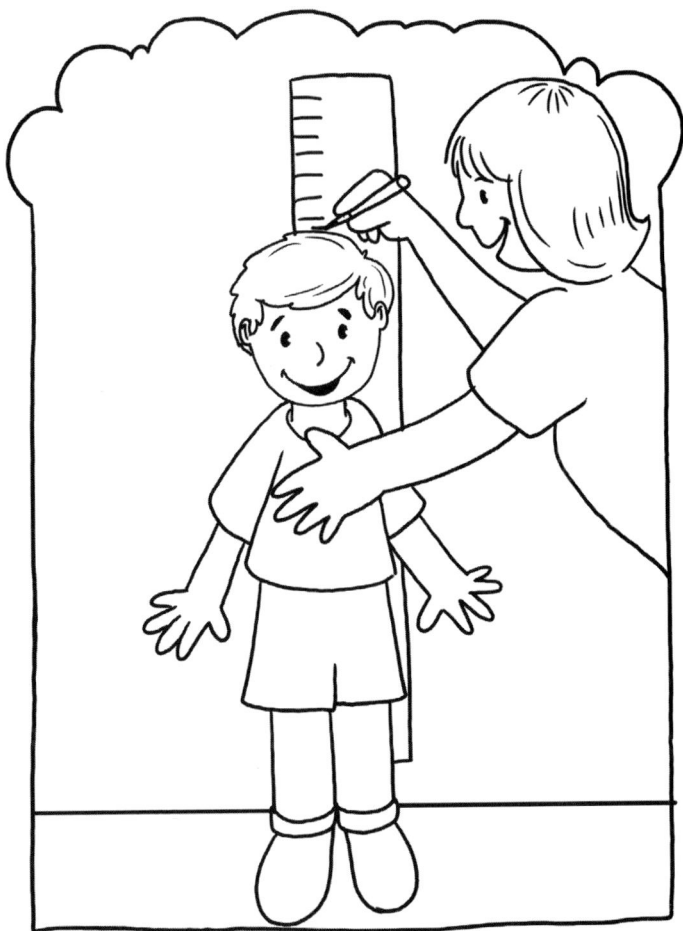

Mom thinks I'm always taller
at the end of a long summer.
I think it's because I
run free on sunny days
through the nice green grass.

When August ends,
fall will start.
First, the winds get cooler.
One leaf falls and then more come
down until no leaves are left.

I wait for the cool fall
and cold winter to pass.
I wait for the snow to melt
and the ground to thaw.

Then it happens.
The sun shines longer.
The grass grows again.
Summer is back!
It's time for more fun in the sun.

Hide and Seek!

Written by Hannah Bayer
Illustrated by Dan Vick

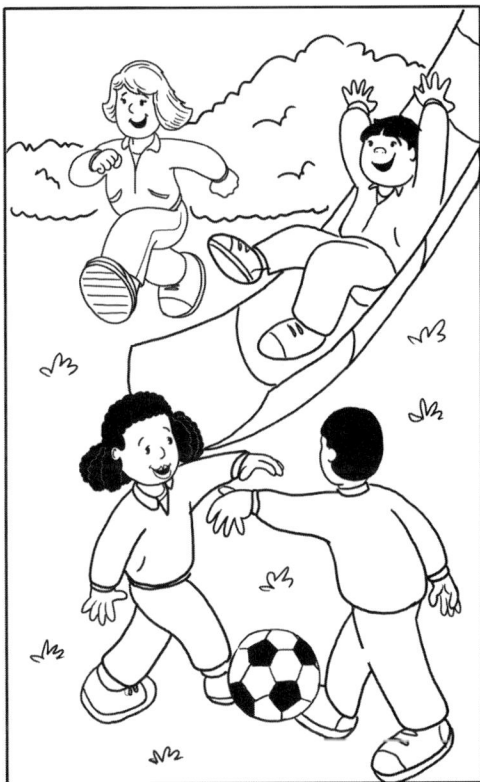

Phonics Skill

Contractions 're, 've, 'd; Irregular Contractions

don't	won't	we're	we've	you're
you've	they're	should've	she'd	

A bell rang in the hall.
"Have fun," called Miss Lee.
"Don't return late!"
"We won't be late," Jen answered.
"We're never late!"

"What can we play?" asked Bobby.
"Let's play tag!" answered Jen.
"We've played that twice this
week," said Tom.
"You're right," said Jen.

"Let's play hide and seek then,"
Fran said.
"That'll be fun!" yelled Kelly.
"I was hoping to play that."

Those kids drew straws
to pick the first seeker.
Jen drew the short straw.
"You've got to count first," said Tom.
"Go hide," Jen called. "I won't peek."

Bobby hid behind the slide.
Tom hid under a bush.
"They've taken all the good spots,"
Fran said to herself.

Fran ducked behind an oak tree
just as Jen finished counting.
Jen found Bobby behind that slide.
"I should've found a better spot,"
Bobby muttered sadly.

Jen found Tom under that bush.
"You're a good seeker," Tom told Jen.
Now where is Fran?
She'd run to base. Fran won!
She'd found the perfect spot.

Mom's Surprise

Written by Renee McLean
Illustrated by Gill Ross

Phonics Skill

Adding Endings -s, -ed, -ing, -er, -est

longest	planning	biggest	returns	tried
excited	helped	prettiest	tied	nicer
pointed	thinking	cleaned	cooking	making
likes	hopped	going	waved	faster
cried	rushed	peeking	called	closed
opened	nicest	hugged		

Mom was on the longest trip.
Ben and Jake are planning the
biggest surprise for when she returns.
They have tried to keep it a secret.
They are so excited!

Dad helped Ben gather the
prettiest flowers in the garden.
Ben tied the bundle.
He set his flowers on the table.

Jake put nicer soaps
in Mom's bathroom.
"Maybe she will enjoy a bubble bath,"
Jake pointed out.
"That is good thinking," Ben said.

Jake and Ben cleaned
while Dad was cooking.
"Dad is a good cook," Jake said.
"I hope he is making what Mom likes."
Jake went to talk to Dad.

Dad, Ben, and Jake hopped
in the car.
They were going to pick up Mom!
She waved faster at them.
"It's Mom!" Jake and Ben cried.

94

They rushed home.
"No peeking!" Ben called.
Mom closed her eyes
as Ben and Jake led her inside.
Then she opened her eyes wide.

"This is the nicest surprise!
When I go away, I like coming
home the best!" Mom cried.
Ben and Jake hugged her tightly.

I Might Be

Written by Greg Morton
Illustrated by Brad Williams

Phonics Skill

Common Syllables -tion, -ture

future	picture(s)	mixture
action	stations	nation
locations	nature	motion

There are many jobs
that people have.
When I think about my future,
I try to picture what I might be.
I have many choices!

Maybe I will be an artist.
I can paint fine pictures,
using a mixture of colors.
My pictures will make people smile.

Maybe I will be a firefighter.
I can take action to protect
my city.
Maybe I will work at stations
all over the nation!

Maybe I will be a builder.
I can make skyscrapers
and houses in many locations.
I could even make a house
for myself!

Maybe I will be a park ranger.
I can see wild animals
and enjoy nature.
I will show people how to be safe
and keep things clean in my park.

Maybe I will be a dancer.
I will be in motion every day.
I will dance in shows
and teach kids
how to move nicely.

My future might hold anything!
I know that I will be happy
if I do something that I like
and that makes other people glad.

Sandy and Randy

Written by Liz Hornby
Illustrated by Vince DePinto

Phonics Skill

Suffixes -ness, -less

useless	sadness	helpless	darkness
kindness	goodness	sweetness	weakness
brightness	colorless		

This is moving day.
Sandy did not grab Randy,
her old bunny doll,
when she ran out the door.

"Did you pack that bunny?"
Mom asked Sandy.
"He's not old and useless."
It filled Sandy with sadness to
know that she left Randy.

"Randy is helpless without me!"
Sandy cried.
"Without me his life will be filled
with darkness and sadness."

"Please show kindness," Sandy begged.
"Let me go back for my bunny."
Mom's goodness shone through.
She smiled because of
Sandy's sweetness.

"You know my weakness,"
Mom laughed. "We won't
leave Randy helpless.
We will go get him."

Sandy picked up Randy and hugged him.
Brightness had come back to her face.
"We'll make you new clothes," she said.
"Your old ones are colorless."

Sandy got in the car
and set Randy on her lap.
Mom smiled.
Mom knew that Sandy would have
missed her good friend.

Hiking the Hard Way

Written by Lynn South
Illustrated by Shannon O'Hara

Phonics Skill
Prefixes mid-, mis-

mismatched	midway	mislaid	misstep
midstream	midday	misplaced	

Danny was so excited!
His scout troop was going hiking.
He loaded his backpack.
But things started going wrong
right away.

Danny put on his boots
in the darkness.
When he got on the bus,
Danny looked down.
His boots were mismatched!

Midway through the bus trip,
Danny cried, "No, no!"
He had mislaid his water bottle.
It was not in his backpack.
"I have two bottles," Kim said.

At the start of that hike,
they crossed a stream.
Danny took a misstep
and slipped midstream.
Splash! Danny got soaked.

Danny dried off
as they hiked on.
The hikers stopped
at midday for lunch.
Danny was happy to stop.